SEX TRICKS EVERY MAN SHOULD MASTER

HOW TO BECOME AN UNFORGETTABLE LOVER

ANTHONY EKANEM

Made with ♥ on the Notion Press Platform
www.notionpress.com

Contents

Preface

The main aim of this material is to give you a summarized version of 10 different things you should know and do to give you and your partner an unforgettable experience each time you are making love.

In this book, you will learn things like:

- The Five Different Categories of Foreplay
- The Difference Between Linear and Non-linear Foreplay
- Foreplay Tips to turn her on
- Erogenous zone on your partner's body and become a master in the art of foreplay
- Kissing techniques that will leave your partner wanting more.
- How to find the G-spot and apply the right techniques to make your partner orgasm
- The sex positions that are best for achieving clitoral and/or vaginal orgasms
- New and exotic yet practical sex positions that will be enjoyable for both you and your partner
- Cunnilingus Techniques that will drive your partner wild and make her beg you for more

- Cunnilingus Exercises and positions to perform like a pro

CHAPTER ONE

Foreplay Techniques

Master the art of foreplay and keep your partner always guessing with anticipation. When we think of foreplay, we only consider the physical act of sexual foreplay. However, what happens before that? Did you know that flirting with another person could be considered foreplay? Why? Because it creates anticipation and that is exactly what foreplay is meant to do. It arouses you and your partner and creates awareness of each other and anticipation of what is to come.

Foreplay can be divided into five categories as follows:

1. Emotional Foreplay
2. Mental Foreplay
3. Practical Foreplay
4. Self-Directed Foreplay
5. Physical Foreplay

EMOTIONAL FOREPLAY

This type of foreplay occurs at any time other than during sexual intercourse. It takes the form of a continual reminder of affection and attraction between you and your partner.

Calling her or sending her text messages during the day just to say you love her or greeting her after the working day with a sincere hug and kiss all form part of emotional foreplay. By practising this form of foreplay, your partner will feel safe within the relationship and is more willing and open to new and exciting sexual experiences with you. This means a lot to a woman.

MENTAL FOREPLAY

If you want your partner to know that you're in the mood for sex now or later when the two of you are alone, this is the type of foreplay to be deployed.

Dirty phone calls or text messages to each other while at work can also be very exciting. Leaving sexy messages helps to create the mood for mind-blowing sex after the two of you get together.

If you think you do not know how to do this, just get started with any funny thing that comes to your mind. Very soon, better, and creative ideas will come to you.

PRACTICAL FOREPLAY

Have you ever wanted to engage in sexual intercourse with your partner, but she was too concerned about the chores that had to be completed first? Worrying about these chores can put one off sex for that evening.

This is where practical foreplay comes in. You know exactly what your partner may put up as an excuse for not having sex and you make sure you go ahead of her and remove all those things. For instance, how about tidying up the house and getting the kids ready for bed. This shows her that you are willing to share the load when it comes to the household as well as ensure that she has enough energy and sustained excitement for a satisfying round of sex.

SELF DIRECTED FOREPLAY

In this form of foreplay, your partner specifies different things to do either for your benefit or her own. These things could include taking baths with scented candles together or wearing sexy lingerie, which is very exciting for the both of you. A lot of couples are mainly African and they do not bathe together. So, trying something like this might be a great turn on.

One rule – never rush your partner at this stage. When she is ready, you will know.

PHYSICAL FOREPLAY

This is the type of foreplay that occurs directly before sexual intercourse. At this stage, you will use different means to bring your partner to sexual readiness. I am going to share some ideas with you.

Massage Her

Women love to be massaged, especially around sensitive areas such as the back, behind the knees and thighs and the feet. You can put some gentle oil on your finger to allow your fingers to glide smoothly over the skin. Watch her reactions carefully and adjust the pressure accordingly.

Kiss Her

Most women will tell you that kissing is one of the most sensual sensations to experience. Concentrate on the mouth, neck, navel, and inner thighs – it will drive her wild!

Nibbling

Gentle nibbles (not bites) can also drive your partner into ecstasy when combined with kissing or sucking on the targeted areas. Zone in on the earlobes as well as the back, inner thighs, and buttocks (some women might need persuasion here but believe me, they will never regret it).

Linear and Non-Linear Foreplay

What is the difference between linear and nonlinear foreplay? Well with linear foreplay, we follow all the usual steps in foreplay. First, we start with kissing and undressing, and then move on to the breasts and navel, and maybe a bit of oral sex, if you are okay with it, and then full sexual intercourse. Many people may practice this form of sexuality because it leads up to the main thing in measured steps. Some may find this boring, unappealing, and unimaginative.

With non-linear foreplay, what you do is to scramble the order of the usual foreplay steps. It is all about creativity and unpredictability. This is going to be exciting for you and your partner because what leads to boring sex life is that as couples become permanent sexual partners, foreplay and intercourse tends to become a routine they can predict. This can create boredom within the relationship.

Changing the order of foreplay in conjunction with new positions can bring new excitement into the relationship. That is why I always talk about Variety. Just change things and don't get too used to a certain way of doing things such that your partner now knows what you want to do before you even do it. When your partner is expecting you to follow "logical" steps with foreplay and you do the unexpected, it shows her that you are spontaneous and adventurous.

Some More Foreplay Tips to Turn Her On

Here are four foreplay tips that you can include in your sex life that will have your woman you seduce begging for satisfaction.

Talk and tease

During foreplay, the power of suggestion (especially with some dirty talk) can be as great as the sex itself for many women. If you can describe how you want to touch her, where and with which of your body parts, she'll visualize it easily and eagerly. If you know how to have sex with her brain (it is a major sexual organ), you can bet that she'll be begging you to have sex with the rest of her in due time.

Get started in public

Foreplay doesn't need to be restricted to the bedroom or inside four walls. If you show her that she turns you on via PDA, when you finally do find yourselves in a private situation, the good times will lead to some carnal indulgences.

Undress Each Other

Undressing one another slowly when you are about to have sex adds some taste to the whole show. I do recommend that you remove your clothes slowly.

You can do it by removing her top first and she does the same thing to you, and you keep following that thread until you are both naked. You may also completely undress her first while she does the same thing to you as well. Also, in this case, undress her just as slowly. Sit her down and remove her clothing one after the other.

Use your fingers and give her oral pleasure

Every woman is different and, therefore, every woman likes to be touched differently. However, there are a lot of techniques that are effective for most women. Bring your hand to her vaginal area and, with the tips of your fingers, rub her outer lips (labia majora) by spreading them apart and bringing them back together. That should start the lubrication process.

When she spreads her legs a bit, that's a clear indication that she wants you to touch her a little deeper. At this point, you can start lightly by rubbing her inner lips (labia minora), and then move up to her clitoris, which you should rub in a circular motion.

Some women like their clitoris to be touched gently, while others prefer a more vigorous contact. If you are both new to it, read her body language for a sign of what you should do. After a few minutes, bring your mouth to the area and, while you continue to use your fingers to play around inside her, gently suck on her clitoris to give her some great oral pleasure.

Always keep things lively, fun, and erotic, and she'll be wanting more. Always remember that every woman is different and if you're attentive, you should be a success.

CHAPTER TWO

A Woman's Erogenous Zones

Still on the issue of foreplay. Hope I am not boring you with it? If you truly want to satisfy a woman, you must know this stuff. That is why I keep approaching it from various angles. What are erogenous zones and where are they found on the body?

Erogenous zones are areas on the body where there is a higher concentration of nerve endings and where these nerve endings are concentrated closer to the skin surface. These zones are activated or aroused either by gentle stroking with fingertips or by massaging the area. Here are some that I want to share with you in this report:

The Neck

This is one of the most sensitive spots on a women's body. If you target this area, it is like unlocking the door to her sexuality. Keep your mouth moderately moist and warm. Kiss or nibble this area gently.

The Ears

There is a high concentration of nerve endings around the ears and especially the earlobes. Gentle nibbles on the lobes will drive many women crazy. Use your tongue to gently tickle the ear while exhaling warm air. Please do not shove your wet tongue down your ear if you want to avoid an abrupt ending to this session. Most women cannot stand it.

The Lips

Many women complain that there is not enough kissing during foreplay and sex. What many men forget is that the lips are extremely sensitive. Start by gently brushing your lips over hers and then move on to gentle French kissing steadily increasing the intensity depending on her reaction.

The Scalp

Massaging the scalp can be very sensual. Just remember to combine this either with kissing or full-on sex. Why? This is a very relaxing activity, and she might drift into a semi-hypnotic sleep if you work on it alone. Not all women like having their heads touched so start slowly and pay careful attention to her reaction when doing this the first time.

The Breasts & Nipples

This area is flush with nerve endings and most men will pay attention to this area. The secret here is soft touches with the fingers, lips, and tongue. The best way to stimulate this area is from the outside in. Start your way at the outer regions of the breast and slowly make your way to the nipples. Don't be in a rush to get there. You want to tease your partner with this action so do your best to resist her prompting. It will drive her crazy!

The Clitoris

This organ is located at the top of the inner vaginal lips. It is a small knob of pink flesh that is covered by a hood. The amount of preferred direct stimulation differs from woman to woman. Always start slowly and gently adjust according to her reaction. With her prompting, you can increase the intensity of the stimulation.

The back of the knees

The area at the back of the knees also has a high concentration of nerve endings. Light caressing with the fingertips or tongue is sure to result in goose pimples.

Her Back & Buttocks

These are also sensitive spots on the body, but not as sensitive as the breast. This is because of the inclusion of muscle in this equation. Gentle caressing with the fingertips or tongue will be enough for the small of the back, but as you move down to the buttocks, the intensity will need to increase. Be sure to pay attention to these all areas during foreplay. The results can only be positive. Be careful not to only go for the breasts like most men do and ignore everything else. Show some creativity and reap the rewards.

CHAPTER THREE

Kissing Techniques

Let me give you some tips here. In life, it is said that first impressions are lasting impressions, and these usually determine whether you take the next step. The same can be said for sex. Kissing is often the first impression your partner will have of you as a lover. In other words, it is your greeting card. If you can kiss her very well, you will move to the next stage. Here are some tips on how to be a good kisser.

The Lip Brush

Use your lips to gently brush over your partner's lips, ears, neck, and nipples. At the same time, breathe deeply and slowly let out hot air through your nose. The combination of hot air and brush is extremely sensual and arousing.

The Tongue Probe

Not everyone woman likes to have a tongue shoved down their throat. Rather start with the tongue gently moving around the entrance of your partner's lips. Then gently probe your partner's mouth in slow rhythmic movements. Your partner will let you know how much of your tongue is welcome.

Once inside, use gently thrusting movements in and out of the mouth ensuring that you can feel her lips around your tongue.

The Tongue Stretch

While French kissing, stretch your tongue so that the tip reaches the roof of your lover's mouth. Then move the tongue around the roof of the tongue to produce incredible sensations for the receiving partner.

The Flat Lick

While keeping your lips in contact with your partner's body, use the full surface of your tongue to massage the skin while gently sucking on the area. This kiss can be used on the neck, back of the neck, back of the knees, the navel area and of course, the nipples. Try not to produce too much moisture with this technique.

The Tongue Massage

While engaged in French Kissing, use your tongue to massage your partner's tongue. Try massaging the top and side of her tongue, as these are sensitive areas. At the same time, use your lips to massage her lips.

They should always be moving in rhythm with your breathing and body movements. This technique can also be used on the ears, neck, navel, and nipples.

CHAPTER FOUR

How to Find the G-Spot

Finding your partners G-Spot is not as difficult as you may think. However, stimulating the G-Spot is a little trickier than stimulating the clitoris. Let me quickly give you a few tips in finding the G-Spot and helping your partner to achieve great orgasms.

Finding the G-Spot

The location of the G-Spot differs slightly from woman to woman; however, they are generally in the same area. Take your moist finger and insert it into your partner's vagina until you have reached the second knuckle. Your palm should be facing her body.

Bend your finger slightly and feel along the vaginal wall. When you reach a patch the size of a quarter that has a slightly rough or bumpy texture, kind of like spongy, you have found the G-Spot. In some women, the G-Spot feels like rough ridges while in others it feels like little bumps. However, generally, the texture of the G-Spot is not as smooth as the rest of the vaginal wall.

Stimulating the G-Spot

Stimulating the G-Spot is not the same as stimulating the clitoris. Rubbing is not going to produce an orgasm. Rather take your finger and apply constant pressure in rhythmic massages to produce an orgasm. This should be done during foreplay to create the right mood and to ensure maximum stimulation.

You will need to be patient with the G-Spot as it takes a bit more time to produce an orgasm than the clitoris. Stimulating the G-Spot during sex is easy and very exciting for both partners. There are positions like the G-factor that can help you stimulate it during sex.

Take note - Your partner should make sure that she urinates before sexual because, during the stimulation of the G-Spot, she will likely feel the sensations of wanting to urinate. This way she will be comforted by the fact that her bladder is empty, and this relaxation will help her feel comfortable and reach her orgasm.

Now that you have been given tools to find and stimulate your partner's G-Spot. Now take your partner and practice these moves. In this case, practice makes perfect and what's more, it is enjoyable.

CHAPTER FIVE

Sex Positions

Trying out different sex positions is a fun and exciting way for you and your partner to find the best ways for achieving clitoral and vaginal orgasms. This will also help the both of you to explore each other with complete honesty and excitement.

It is generally accepted that face-to-face penetration is great for enhancing clitoral stimulation. This allows your penis to directly stimulate your partner's clitoris. Deeper penetration can also help to stimulate the clitoris if you can position your pelvis in such a manner that the top of your penis or the area above your penis can stimulate your clitoris.

Here are some positions to help stimulate your partner's clitoris: You may have heard about them as well.

The 45 Degree Missionary

Here your partner lies back with her legs flat while you enter her as in the missionary. Then twist yourself to an angle of 45 degrees so that your bodies form an X. The grinding and circular movements of your hips will ensure that her clitoris is sufficiently stimulated to produce a great orgasm.

The Reversed Missionary

This position takes the standard missionary but reverses the roles of both partners. Here, you will lay on your back with your legs open and pulled towards your chest. Your partner then moves in between your legs and pulls your penis into her. She controls the grinding and thrusting while holding up your knees. You can either lie back and enjoy, or you can manually stimulate her clitoris, which should be already directly stimulated by your penis.

The Closed Missionary

This position takes the form of the usual missionary with your laying on the bottom and you on top. However, the difference is that her legs are closed, and your legs are outside of hers.

Using this position allows for direct stimulation of the clitoris as well as a tighter fit for the penis. Both of you are sure to get enhanced orgasms. The best method to achieve vaginal or G-Spot orgasms this way is to use deeper penetration with either face to face or with rear entry.

Here are some positions that will help your partner to achieve vaginal orgasms.

The Rocking Chair

Both of you must sit facing each other; your partner's legs wide open and yours also open but within hers. You will enter her and then you grab each other's arms. Both of you move in a rocking motion which stimulates her G-spot with constant pressure nudges. Continuing with this long enough will produce a great orgasm.

Doggy Style Raised

In this position, your partner starts on all fours. You then enter her from behind and then lift her legs off the bed or ground. She then wraps her presses them against your buttocks. This allows for deep penetration but can also target the G-spot ensuring great orgasms for both partners.

Try practising these positions over some time and they will come more naturally and will become a permanent feature of your sex life.

Exotic Sex Positions That Will Be Enjoyable For both You and Your Partner

Spicing up your sex life does not need to be hard labour for you and your partner. It should be a fun experience for both of you. Trying out new and exotic positions should ideally take place once you and your partner have gotten to know and trust each other. This way, you will both be open to trying out new sexual acts. The ones that would excite you! Here are some new positions that could be enjoyed by both of you.

You on Top - **The Deep Drill**

Here, your partner lies on her back and rests her legs on your shoulder. You will then penetrate her while in a kneeling position. Using this position allows for deep and hard thrusting penetration which no doubt will be enjoyable for you. By changing the angle of the thrust, you will be able to stimulate either the clitoris or the G-Spot, which is great for her.

She on Top - **Rodeo Girl**

You will lay on your back with your knees bent. Your partner will then squat on top of you while remaining on her feet. She can lean back against your knees for support. You will benefit from a tighter fit, which drives most men crazy. She also gains by controlling the angle and the rate of the thrust. This assures her of either clitoral or vaginal orgasms.

The Spider

In this position, you lay on your back with your legs flat on the bed. Your partner then crawls on top of your head on hands and feet but facing upwards. You then penetrate her from behind. The wonderful thing about this position is that both of you can thrust. Should she get tired, all she must do is to lower herself on top of you and let you carry on doing the work.

Your partner also gets to control the penetration. For deep thrusts, she simply arches her back and for shallow penetration, she straightens her back. She decides whether she wants you to stimulate her clitoris or G-spot.

The Ironing Board

Use a chair or coffee table for this. Let your partner face the table and lay over it with her knees on the ground and keep her back as straight as possible. You will then penetrate her from the back. If she closes her legs, you will benefit from a tighter fit.

The Wall Banger

This is a rear-entry penetration. Your partner faces and leans against the wall. You will then come in behind her and penetrate her while adjusting her hips. Your partner can adjust the angle of her pelvis so that your penis hits the G-Spot, which is very satisfying for her. Now that you have learned these exciting positions, take your partner and practice each of them slowly.

CHAPTER SIX

Cunnilingus Techniques

You can skip this if you think it is not okay for you. I also used to have a negative idea about this before but that has changed now but we are all entitled to our opinions and my job is not to change yours. A great way to show your partner that you care about her sexual satisfaction is to perform oral sex or cunnilingus on her if she is okay with it. It makes her feel that she is the centre of your universe because you would do anything to make sure that she is satisfied.

Here are the oral techniques I want to share with you here.

The Ice-cream Lick

Imagine yourself licking a cone of ice cream with a soft flat tongue. The same principle is applied to licking the clitoris. This should be done from the vaginal entrance towards on over the clitoris, always in an upward motion. This technique should also be applied along the outer regions of the vagina keeping the tongue as flat and moist as possible. Remember most of the nerve endings are in the outer regions of the vagina.

The Envelope Lick

When you need to seal an envelope, you would lick the edges. The same can be done with the vaginal lips with a difference. Using your lips, hold the vaginal lips together while running your tongue between the inner and outer labia. Do this one side at a time.

The Flickering Tongue

Use your fingers to spread the vaginal lips apart. Then use your tongue to lightly flick over your partner's vagina. Increase the intensity of the flick as her excitement increases. Remember to always keep your tongue as moist as possible. If this proves too intense for her, stop immediately as it can become painful.

The Clitoris Vacuum

This technique is done by exposing the clitoris and gently pulling it into your mouth. Suck on the clitoris with very gentle in and out movement with the aid of your tongue. The sensations of this action are very intense so you should be always very aware of your partner's reaction. If things get too much for her, stop immediately. If on the other hand she enjoys it then increase the suction very, very slightly.

Tongue Intercourse

As mentioned previously in this report, most woman's nerve endings are in the outer regions of the vagina. These nerves are easily accessible with the tongue. Use your tongue in a thrusting and swirling motion to stimulate these nerves. Your partner's reaction will be pleasantly surprising. Practice these techniques with your partner regularly and see how she rewards you in return.

Cunnilingus Exercises and Positions to Help You Perform Like a Pro

The art of cunnilingus (using your tongue on a woman) needs to be practised, and practice makes perfect. Once you have the hang of it, you will never lose this skill, and this skill is one that women admire. The main aim of these exercises is to improve the dexterity and maneuverability of the tongue.

It is of course the tongue that performs the main function in stimulating the clitoris. The four practical exercises detailed below will help bring the mouth and tongue to peak physical condition to provide sensual stimulation of the clitoris and vagina.

Exercise 1:

Start by sticking your tongue out as far as you can. Now curl your tongue upwards and try to touch the tip of your nose with the tip of your tongue and hold it there for 10 seconds. Now swirl your tongue around in a clockwise direction always meeting back up with the nose. Repeat this 10 times and then reverse the direction of the swirl and repeat 10 times. When swirling the tongue, try to move it as far as you can in different directions. In other words, exaggerated movements.

Exercise 2:

As with exercise 1, stick out your tongue and try to touch the tip of your nose with the tip of your tongue. Now move your tongue down and try to touch your chin while flattening your tongue. Repeat this motion 20 times while increasing the reach of your tongue with each repetition.

Exercise 3:

Relax your jaw and your top lip. Now flick your relaxed tongue in and out of your mouth while always making sure that your tongue flicks across your top lip. Start with about 100 flicks per minute then increase the rate of flicking as fast as you can. Do this for 30 seconds at a time. Notice how your lip starts to tingle? Now just imagine what this does for the clitoris and the labia of the woman.

Exercise 4:

Stick out your tongue while keeping it flat. The sides of your tongue should be touching the top lip. Now try to curl up the sides of the tongue to form a tube. If needed, use the top lips to assist the tongue to form the tube. Once the tube has been formed, move your tongue in and out between your lips. Do this for about 30 seconds at a time. The purpose of this exercise is to allow the tongue to envelop the clitoris and be able to use thrusting motions over this organ to provide the most intense sensations.

All the above exercises should be done in sets of three. Doing these exercises regularly will help your tongue to become the real love machine in your sex life.

9 798889 517429

Printed by Libri Plureos GmbH in Hamburg,
Germany